SENT

SENT

Delivering the Gift of Hope at Christmas

Jorge Acevedo
with Jacob Armstrong, Rachel Billups, Justin LaRosa & Lanecia Rouse

Abingdon Press
Nashville

Sent
Delivering the Gift of Hope at Christmas
Large Print Edition

ISBN 978-1-5018-0105-1

15 16 17 18 19 20 21 22 23 24—10 9 8 7 6 5 4 3 2 1

CONTENTS

Introduction
Jorge Acevedo 7

1. Jesus Reconciles
Jacob Armstrong.....................................11

2. Jesus Sets Us Free
Lanecia Rouse 33

3. Jesus Is God With Us
Justin LaRosa..55

4. Jesus Brings New Life
Rachel Billups 75

5. Jesus Changes Everything
Jorge Acevedo 97

Notes 107

INTRODUCTION

JORGE ACEVEDO

In the summer of 2013, my wife Cheryl and I were in England during the much-anticipated birth of Prince George, son of Prince William and Duchess Kate. The British people's excitement about the birth of the monarch was at a fever pitch. It monopolized the media and the minds of a nation. The young prince was born on July 22, 2013, at St. Mary's Hospital in London. His official birth announcement, following royal tradition, was placed on an easel outside Buckingham Palace: "Her Royal Highness The Duchess of Cambridge was safely delivered of a son at 4:24 p.m. today. Her Royal Highness and her child are both doing well."

The first Christmas was the complete opposite of Prince George's royal birth. No media were present. Joseph didn't tweet out details of their seventy-mile journey from Nazareth to Bethlehem. Mary didn't have a Facebook page where she could show off pictures of her newborn son. CNN and Fox News weren't there to provide moment-by-moment updates on the Savior's birth. Yet what happened that first Christmas revolutionized planet Earth more than the birth of any monarch before or since. This world still hasn't gotten over the birth of Jesus.

It was the great wisdom of our early church fathers and mothers to set aside the four weeks before Christmas to prepare for Jesus' birth, in the season we call Advent. The word *advent* means "arrival" or "coming." What our forefathers and foremothers understood was that Jesus' birth was not just a one-time occurrence, but that every Christmas has within it the possibility of Jesus being born again in our lives and in our world. Historically Jesus' birth happened once, but spiritually his birth can happen anew for us today.

I love the way the Christmas carols have deep spiritual truths embedded in their lyrics. Check out this powerful verse from the well-known carol "O Little Town of Bethlehem."

> O holy Child of Bethlehem,
> descend to us, we pray;
> cast out our sin, and enter in,
> be born in us today.

We hear the Christmas angels
the great glad tidings tell;
O come to us, abide with us.
our Lord Emmanuel![1]

"Cast out our sin, and enter in, be born in us today." Where does Christ need to be born in you today? One of my mentors, Bishop Dick Wills, used to say that if you can't tell someone what God has done in your life during the last thirty days, you may not have a relationship with God. Dick was arguing for an "up-to-date" faith, a faith constantly being born and reborn in our lives.

In this book, I've invited four friends—Jacob, Lanecia, Justin, and Rachel—to join me in telling some very special stories about the way Jesus was reborn in their lives. You'll go to Waffle House. You'll meet Ruby. You'll greet a brand-new baby. You'll hear about a Christmas tree skirt. You'll spend a restless night, then wake up Googling.

Two thousand years ago, a baby was born who changed the world. God sent Jesus, and today, you and I are sent to be his hands and feet, delivering God's gift of hope to a world in need.

Let's begin our Advent journey together!

We hear the Christmas angels
the great glad tidings tell;
O come to us, abide with us,
our Lord Emmanuel!

"Cast out our sin, and enter in, be born in us today." Where does Christ need to be born in you today? One of my mentors, Bishop Dick Wills, used to say that if you can't tell someone what God has done in your life during the last thirty days, you may not have a relationship with God. I think he was getting at an up-to-date, keen faith constantly being born and reborn in our lives.

In this book, I've invited four friends—Jacob, Lauren, Justin, and Rachel—to join me in telling some very special stories about the way Jesus was reborn in their lives. You'll go to Waffle House. You'll meet Ruby. You'll greet a brand-new baby. You'll hear about a Christmas tree skirt. You'll spend a restless night, then wake up Googling.

Two thousand years ago, a baby was born who changed the world. God sent Jesus, and today, you and I are sent to be his hands and feet, delivering God's gift of hope to a world in need.

Let's begin our Advent journey together!

1. JESUS RECONCILES

JACOB ARMSTRONG

In that region there were shepherds living in the fields, keeping watch over their flock by night. Then an angel of the Lord stood before them, and the glory of the Lord shone around them, and they were terrified. But the angel said to them, "Do not be afraid; for see—I am bringing you good news of great joy for all the people."

(Luke 2:8-10 NRSV)

The Waffle House

A few years ago, during Advent, my two older daughters asked me a question I wasn't expecting: "Dad, will you ever take us to Waffle House?"

Mary and Lydia were eight and six years old at the time, and I had never taken them to Waffle House. I hold nothing against Waffle House—in fact, I kind of like it—but it was true, I had never taken them there. My two girls had seen this strange little building in the middle of their world, and naturally they had wondered, *What takes place in this mysterious house of waffles?* Without thinking twice, I said, "Yes, we will get up early before school and go."

There was one problem. We had not received all the necessary permissions. So, we gathered together and formed our argument and then went to present our case before their mother: "We will go to bed early, we'll have our clothes set out, no complaining, no grumbling, this will be a seamless operation." And after some deliberation, she said...yes.

The night before our excursion, the local weather report said it was going to snow. I envisioned it in my mind: We would venture through the snow, a dad and his daughters on a memorable but dangerous journey, and finally make it to Waffle House with a few harrowing moments along the way. We would sit at a table by the big window and look out at a snowcapped shopping mall. Deer would dance through the Red Lobster parking lot. It would be magical.

Well, I woke up the next morning (it had not snowed), and it turns out that at five a.m. our house is totally devoid of magic. When I tried to wake the girls, they grumbled. When I reminded them of our plan, they kept right on sleeping. My plan was falling apart before my eyes.

"Hey, I went to bed at seven o'clock last night," I exclaimed. "We are going to Waffle House!" I roused them, and off we went.

On the ride over, from the back seat, Lydia said something that let me know the morning's adventure might be a story that I would still tell years later.

"Daddy, I don't feel normal."

"What do you mean, you don't feel normal?" I asked.

She replied, "You know—it's dark, we're going to a restaurant when usually we'd be getting ready for school. It just doesn't feel normal."

"Well," I said, "sometimes when you do something you don't normally do, you see something you don't normally see."

Pretty good line, Jake, I thought, especially at 5:45 a.m. So I said it again.

"Sometimes when you do something you don't normally do, you see something you don't normally see."

We walked into Waffle House before the sun had risen, two little girls wearing pink jackets in a place otherwise packed with men wearing work boots and drinking coffee.

We sat by the window. Cars were zooming by, hundreds of cars, headlights reflecting on the darkened streets. Mary asked, "Where are all these people going? Who are they, driving around in the dark?" I said "They're going to work, or coming back from work. In fact, these ladies who served us breakfast had to get up early to be here." Our server overheard our conversation. "Sugar," she said, "I've been here since 10:30 last night."

My daughters and I thought of all the people who work while we snooze. We talked about nurses, truck drivers, police officers, moms who stay up all night with kids—there's this whole world going on while we're asleep. We talked about our servers who had been here, unbeknownst to us, all night long.

Well, Waffle House was everything we had hoped for—waffles, sausage, hash browns, scattered, smothered, and covered. And it was then, a week before Christmas, that I saw something I don't normally see: God's people living and working at night. It hit me that the first people who got the news about the baby—the Messiah, the great Reconciler who would come and save us—the first ones were a bunch of shepherds, guys working the graveyard shift in the middle of the night. God wanted them to know that the good news was for them, so much so that God chose them to be the ones to hear the news first. The baby was born and wrapped in swaddling clothes, and God told the shepherds first. Not God made sure all the kings of all the great empires knew first that the Savior had come to Bethlehem. Nope. Not God went to the Temple and let all the priests who had given their lives to God be the first to know of the great arrival. Not what it says. The Bible tells us there were shepherds working at night, and the glory of the Lord shone around them.

And I wondered, if that grand announcement came tonight, would God go to Waffle House while it was still dark and tell the ladies who work all night?

Why Us?

As we might imagine, the shepherds were surprised they were chosen to receive this message. Notice the use of the word *you* in the angels' announcement. "I bring *you* good news of great joy." The Savior "has been born to *you*." It was happening in their town, and they were the ones being told. Surely they wondered, *Why us?*

Jesus Comes to the Unsuspecting

This seems to be a key ingredient in those God chooses. They don't see it coming! They don't see themselves as the ones God would want or choose.

Zechariah and Elizabeth were counting the days until retirement. Mary was living her life in Nazareth, a town in Galilee, a virgin pledged to marry a man named Joseph. Read into that: they were nothing special. The shepherds were just at work on just another night. Jesus was sent to them. And none of them saw it coming.

Jesus Comes to the Unqualified

The first things that the key players in the Christmas story thought of when told that Jesus was coming into their lives were all the reasons why they should not receive such news. Zechariah said, "I'm an old man!" Mary asked, "How can this be? I am a virgin." We don't hear the shepherds' response, but as normal working folk surely they felt unqualified to receive and then share the message.

When I first asked my bishop if I could start a church, I gave the worst sales pitch ever. I began by listing all the reasons I shouldn't be the one to do it. I was twenty-five, I had never pastored a church, the list went on. He said, "You're right. However, God does not call the equipped but equips the called." You may have heard that line before, but it rings true. God doesn't call the ones who have all the equipping and qualifications. But God does give the called all they need.

Jesus Comes to the Undeserving

The shepherds were not chosen because they met certain criteria or had lived up to a standard. These weren't the best shepherds in town. They weren't the most successful. They did not have a prestigious bloodline. These were not the shepherds who had won the Bethlehem's Choice award for most popular in their field. We revere them now, along with many others from the traditional Advent Scriptures, but they were as undeserving as we are to be recipients of world-changing news. We miss some of the Christmas story's power if we neglect to see that the shepherds were unsuspecting, unqualified, and undeserving to be included. And God picked them anyway.

Jesus Was Sent for All People

Jesus came for all people, and nowhere is this more evident than the birth narrative in Luke 2. This short passage is the foundation for many things we have come to associate with Christmas. From Nativity scene figurines on the mantle to children dressing up like shepherds in the pageant to Linus's reading of the story in *A Charlie Brown Christmas,* we have Luke to thank for many things that have come to mean and feel like Christmas. Yet a close reading of Luke's version of the story shows that his intent was not to give a warm, fuzzy feeling to folks two thousand years later during a holiday season. Luke wanted the world to know: Jesus was sent for all people.

And if Jesus was sent for all people, Jesus was sent for you. Perhaps you can see yourself in the story. In Luke 2 alone, we glimpse some of the people Jesus was sent for:

- Those whose expectations for their lives have changed
- Those who find themselves physically uncomfortable
- Those who drive crowded streets
- Those who feel that they live where they work
- Those who are afraid, even terrified
- Those who need good news
- Those who are in a hurry

- Those who are amazed by some things happening in their life
- Those who are pondering and processing some things happening in their lives

Jesus, in short, was sent for people who felt and experienced the same things we do. They were a people in need, a people who were desperate for help; they were people just like us.

Jesus Was Sent to Reconcile

When we use the word *reconcile*, there is the implication that something that once had been will be restored. Someone or something will be brought back, and things will be made right. Jesus was sent to reconcile. His purpose was to restore something that once had been, and all the people in Luke 2 were longing for it. All the people driving by Waffle House in the dark are longing for it. I am longing for it. You are longing for it.

Our Longing, God's Longing

There is this thing that happens at Christmas that fascinates me. All year long we've been grown up. We've rushed from appointment to appointment, paid the bills, been responsible, sensible, and stressed out—well, you know all the things we do.

Then suddenly, around the end of Thanksgiving, something awakens in us. We put lights up on the house, animatronic deer in the yard, life-size snow globes of Santa on our front lawns. We listen to music that we heard as kids. We pile into the car and drive around the neighborhood to look at lights. We put on ugly Christmas sweaters and drink eggnog. We don't just give people gifts; we wrap the gifts in fancy paper.

Our hearts seem to wake up, and by the time we get to Christmas Eve we are deeply, deeply longing for something more. On Christmas Eve night at our church, we pack into a musty middle-school gym for worship. We listen to the story once again. You know the story, the one from Luke 2, the one about great joy for all the people. The story of the amazing child sent by God to answer every longing of our hearts. A baby sent to reconcile us back to where we hoped we might return. The story is not just about a baby, though. It is about a young, unmarried couple and rich kings. It is about an old couple who thought their dream was over. It is about shepherds working the third shift.

And on Christmas Eve, after the story, we turn off all the lights, then one by one, hand to hand, we light candles and sing.

> Silent night, holy night,
> shepherds quake at the sight;
> glories stream from heaven afar,
> heavenly hosts sing Alleluia!

Christ the Savior is born,
Christ the Savior is born![1]

Advent is a beautiful time, even if you get frustrated with the commercialization and the busyness of it all. There is something beautiful happening in the hearts of people who long for something else, who hope that we will find what our hearts yearn for. In my estimation we are hoping and longing for reconciliation. And the longing is deep.

One way to describe the longing is to think of a child wanting that one special gift. It seems every year there is that one gift everyone has to have. The Red Ryder BB gun from the movie *A Christmas Story* immediately comes to mind. Or perhaps you remember the craze around the Tickle Me Elmo toy in 1996. Or does anyone remember Furby? Before we assign this type of longing to children only, let's admit that some of us have stood in line for the newest iPhone. We all feel longing, and at times we will stop at nothing to get what we long for. But there are gifts that can be bought, and there are things that we long for in a deeper way, things for which there is no line and no gift wrapping. It's that feeling that we are hoping can be satisfied at Christmas.

I have mentioned Zechariah and Elizabeth already. Their story is commonly found in the first week of Advent Scripture readings. Zechariah and Elizabeth were longing for a child. That longing and ache is written into their story. Their description in Luke 1 includes family lineage, where Zechariah worked, and, oh yeah, they are old with no children. Their longing became something that defined them.

And then it came time for the priestly division where Zechariah worked to be on duty at the Temple. It was his shift, and Zechariah was chosen by lot to be the one who would go into the Temple and burn incense. This was a big deal. It is possible this could have been the only time Zechariah was asked to do this in his career. Here he was, an old man, counting his days to retirement, and he was chosen. The burning of incense was a way of symbolizing the prayers of God's people being raised up to God. It was more than symbolic, though. Zechariah would be praying, and while he was doing it there would be a large crowd of people assembled just outside to pray as Zechariah did the sacred duty. What were they praying for? The longing of their hearts! The longing of their people! That God would come and make things right, that God would send this Messiah they were waiting for, that God would reconcile. This was their hearts' longing—that God's promise would be fulfilled and would redeem them from oppression, from sin, from the difficulties of life.

So Zechariah went into the Temple, where that day he was the only person allowed to enter, and found that he wasn't alone. God's messenger was there, and the message was for him: "Your prayer has been heard."

My guess is that after Zechariah got over his fear, he must have thought initially that the angel was referring to the people's prayer for reconciliation and a Messiah. But as the angel continued, it finally must have dawned on Zechariah that the angel was speaking to him personally. Your prayer, Zechariah, has been heard. Your longing has reached the ears of God. Your wife Elizabeth will have a son. And this son is going to be the one who will go before the Messiah. Zechariah, the longing of your heart to have a child is connected to the longing of all God's people.

I have learned that often our deepest longing for reconciliation is connected to God's desire for reconciliation with others. The longing that keeps us up at night leads us to be a part of God's longing for the world. Zechariah and Elizabeth, who must have thought that any great part in God's plan had passed them by, suddenly found they were major players in God's reconciliation with all people.

On a recent trip to Los Cerritos, Nicaragua, I found myself crying by a creek. I had made the long walk from the village to the nearest water source. The temperature that day was nearly 100 degrees, and the walk had brought me near exhaustion. After filling a bucket with contaminated water, I had begun climbing a steep embankment as part of the walk back, and the weight of the water along with my fatigue brought me to my knees. I wept, knowing that day after day the women of Los Cerritos made this walk. Unlike me, they wouldn't board a plane a few days later and fly to a world where I don't have to worry about clean drinking water. I don't fear that my children will die of diarrhea. My daughters will not drop out of school during their elementary years to help their mother with the daily burden of carrying water. I cried, and I prayed, and I felt an intense longing for something different in the lives of those people. In that moment I think I felt the longing of the whole village. I didn't know what to do. Truthfully, there was little I could do.

I learned that for ten thousand dollars, the people in that community could have a clean water well. It seemed like such a small amount compared to the change it would bring. After returning home, I shared my longing with our church. Five minutes after I shared that story, a couple who were coming through the line for Holy Communion handed me a check with that exact amount written on it. It turned out they had been feeling a longing to do something with the provision God had given them. In the weeks that followed, additional tens of thousands of dollars came in from our congregation. Today, the community of Los Cerritos has clean water running through a water system to every home. What I realize now is that the longing I felt at the creek that day was not my own. It wasn't even the longing of the people who lived in that village. It was the longing of God for God's own people. God included me in it, and I am grateful.

What do you long for? To put it another way, where in your life do you need reconciliation?

It's a risky question, because it causes us to be vulnerable before God and probably before other people. Do you long for healing, for a relationship to be restored? Do you long for bills to be paid? Do you ache for forgiveness? Do you ache for a child? Perhaps your longing is for something bigger than yourself, such as peace and reconciliation in places where there is war, racial inequality, or slavery.

The promise of Advent is that God hears our longings, sends Jesus to reconcile us, and then sends us as messengers of that reconciliation. God, through Jesus Christ, wants to come and meet you in your longing. Like me, you might want a new iPhone, but what if we allowed God to wipe the crust off our hearts and instead pay attention to a deeper longing? We were sent to reconcile with God. We were sent to serve God.

Do Not Be Afraid

It should be noted that when we long for what God longs for, seeking reconciliation for ourselves and others, we often will experience a strong emotion—fear.

Right before Zechariah was told, "Your prayer has been heard," the angel said, "Do not be afraid." When Mary was greeted as the highly favored one, she was told the same thing: "Do not be afraid." According to Matthew, when God appeared to Joseph in a dream and was told what role he would have, he likewise was told, "Do not be afraid." And who could forget the shepherds, minding their own business in the middle of the night? They were greeted with, you guessed it, "Do not be afraid."

Why were those the first words of God's heavenly messengers? Because the people they greeted were afraid! Over the years we've made those people out to be our courageous heroes (and rightly so, I think), but their stories begin with the fear that comes when you realize God wants to use you.

The Christmas story is for those who are afraid. It is for old couples who think life has passed them by. It is for pregnant, unwed teenagers. It is for those facing punishment by death. It is for those who fear they won't make it through scary economic times, or their latest diagnosis, or another anxiety-filled day.

This story is for the afraid. The ones whom God sends start out afraid and are reconciled to a God who says to them, over and over again, "Do not be afraid. Do not be afraid. Do not be afraid."

At the age of twenty, I drove myself to an emergency room in the middle of the night. I thought I was having a heart attack. Instead, the doctor said I was having a panic attack. He asked me what I was afraid of. I had no answer. In the days that followed, I realized I was afraid of pretty much everything—growing up, paying bills, facing my longings, the list went on.

I began a journey through the Scriptures that has given me strength to this day. I noted the dozens and dozens of times that God or someone speaking for God said, "Do not be afraid" or some variation of it. For me as a young person who was deeply afraid, it meant I wasn't disqualified from being someone God reconciles and then sends. I was intrigued by a God who told Joshua three times to be courageous. I figured that Joshua, like me, must have needed to hear it more than once.

Who does God say "Do not be afraid" to? Afraid people. Who does God send into the world to do the greatest work? Those same people. In fact, it's not the people bursting with courage and confidence whom God seems to use. Instead, it's the people who are utterly terrified that God is including them in the story. It's the people who thought they would live out their existence on the third shift, unseen by the world and perhaps by God. No, says God, you are going to have an important role in my greatest work, the reconciliation of all people.

The World Needs Reconciliation

We need reconciliation. Our story begins in a garden where the relationship between humans and God was like friends who walked together in the late afternoon. But when both man and woman chose to go their own way rather than the way of God, the close relationship that existed in the garden was suddenly compromised. Though God continually offered that same type of presence and relationship, men and women continued to choose their own way. Through sin and slavery, wilderness and exile, God offered to come near, but the people held on to a fear that led them further away from God. God ultimately promised a Messiah, a Savior, who would come and save the story. The Messiah would reconcile the people back to God. The people waited and waited.

Then, God sent Jesus as a baby in a manger. Everyone who received the news was unsuspecting, unqualified, undeserving. The baby was said to be Immanuel, God with us. Again. Finally.

Sometimes as a pastor I will get a call in the middle of the night—not often, but when I do, I know something is wrong. In the first year of starting Providence Church, I received such a call. I couldn't make out all the words, but I could tell that the person on the other end of the line was very upset. I heard the words *accident*, *hospital*, and *please come*. I determined that two of our teenagers had been in a car accident and had been flown by helicopter to the hospital. I arrived at the hospital in the early hours of the morning, while it was still dark. The lobby, which I had visited many times during the day, lacked the hectic and crowded feeling it had held in the daylight. In the night there was no one there—no one but two sets of parents who feared the worst. In those moments we didn't know the condition of their sons.

There weren't a lot of words as we waited and waited. On a table next to us I noticed a Gideon Bible. I picked it up and began to thumb through it. One of the moms asked if I would read the Scripture we had read on Sunday, two days before. I did.

The LORD is my shepherd...

I thought of a God who stays up all night to watch over us. I continued to read words that were the opposite of how we were feeling.

He makes me lie down in green pastures... he restores my soul....Even though I walk through the valley of the shadow of deaths...

And then, there they were, words that had carried me through my most anxious times, words spoken to countless folks fearing for their lives in the middle of the night.

I fear no evil; for you are with me....

It was still scary, and the families would have months and even years of hard moments coming out of that night—broken necks that had to heal and legs that had to learn to walk again. But I assure you, in that darkest moment in the middle of the night in the hospital lobby, God was with us. Just as God was with Mary in a donkey stall, just as God was with shepherds sleeping on the ground, just as God was with a Waffle House waitress finishing her shift. Immanuel.

Just as God was with them, God is with us. And when the unsuspecting, unqualified, undeserving people of God realize that God has sent Jesus to them, they go and tell others.

> So they hurried off and found Mary and Joseph, and the baby, who was lying in the manger. When they had seen him, they spread the word concerning what had been told them about this child, and all who heard it were amazed at what the shepherds said to them. (Luke 2:16-18 NIV)

The ones to whom Jesus was sent became the ones who were sent to bring Jesus to others. That's the deal.

So this year, when you feel a deep longing at Christmas, think about the baby. Think about reconciliation. Then ask, "Where am I being sent?"

Reflecting: Jesus Reconciles

Jesus was sent to reconcile broken hearts and broken people in a broken world. What are the broken places in your life right now? How does reflecting on the Christmas story and remembering that God is bigger than your circumstances give you hope?

Jesus came to reconcile all people to God. Who are the people God has put before you who need to hear this message?

2. JESUS SETS US FREE

Lanecia Rouse

Jesus went to Nazareth, where he had been raised. On the Sabbath he went to the synagogue as he normally did and stood up to read. The synagogue assistant gave him the scroll from the prophet Isaiah. He unrolled the scroll and found the place where it was written:

The Spirit of the Lord is upon me,
because the Lord has anointed me.
He has sent me to preach good news to the poor,
to proclaim release to the prisoners
and recovery of sight to the blind,
to liberate the oppressed,
and to proclaim the year of the Lord's favor.

(Luke 4:16-19 CEB)

Ms. Ruby

One Christmas Eve a few years ago, I hosted Room in the Inn with my sister, brother-in-law, and a dear friend of ours named Ms. Ruby. Room in the Inn is a national program in which different city churches invite people who are experiencing homelessness to eat a meal and spend the night during the cold months. It was the first time in my five years of serving at this particular church that our host night fell on Christmas Eve. When I heard in staff meeting that our night fell on Christmas Eve and that they needed volunteers, I knew without a doubt there was no other way I would want to celebrate the birth of Jesus Christ.

Immediately following the staff meeting, I texted my sister, Ciona, to see if she was up for being a host with me. Then I made my way to Ms. Ruby's home to talk with her and her caretakers to see if it was something she wanted to do and could do without too much stress.

You have to understand, Ms. Ruby is like family to me, and she was born with intellectual disabilities. Our friendship began when we shared meals together at church, and eventually it evolved into movie dates, porch swing conversations, dance parties on road trips to church retreats, and holidays when Ciona and I had the joy of hosting Ms. Ruby at our house. Christmas that year happened to be one of the holidays when Ms. Ruby was going to be with us.

After receiving the okay from her caretakers, I had a conversation with Ms. Ruby to ask her if she was up for "hosting Jesus" for dinner and staying overnight at church following the Christmas Eve service. She said yes, absolutely delighted at the thought of hosting Jesus.

When Christmas Eve arrived, we were all giddy with joy and anticipation, especially Ms. Ruby. The tables had been set for dinner, the twelve bed mattresses had been prepared, and Ms. Ruby was on the edge of her seat waiting for our guests to arrive. Then the moment came.

"They're here, Ms. Ruby," I told her.

"O-wee!" she yelped. She got out of her chair and quickly walked toward the glass door with her arms opened wide.

As the twelve men filed in, Ruby greeted each one of them with, "Hello, Jesus. Ho, ho, ho!"

Throughout the evening, as she talked with the men, shared a meal with them, and attended to their needs, she called them Jesus. Every now and then during the evening she would let us know how she was doing: "Happy here, Ruby happy here."

I paid close attention to the Christmas story unfolding in the community center that night. There were so many sacred moments. I breathed in the goodness and love of God that flowed through the room, in our guests, the hosts, and those who prepared the meal.

I was most captivated by Ms. Ruby's ability to see Jesus in each of the guests and their ability to see Jesus in her. Her loving spirit brought a smile of joy to each face. She moved around the room, freely offering her presence and friendship with authenticity, acceptance, and unconditional love. It was compelling. Equally as compelling were the kindness, respect, and acceptance the guests extended to Ruby.

There was one moment when she turned to a guest who had just finished singing a Christmas song with her and said, "I love you, Jesus." He looked her and said, "I love you, too, Ms. Ruby."

When it was bedtime and Ms. Ruby noticed all the men settling down on their mattresses for the night, she quietly packed her stuff and got ready to leave, not realizing that hosting Room in the Inn meant sleeping on an airbed on the gym floor.

"Ruby ready," she said, coat on and purse in hand.

"Oh, Ms. Ruby, we're staying here tonight," I said. "We're the hosts, remember?"

She was quiet for a minute, then looked at me and said, "Jesus?"

I replied, "Yes, Ms. Ruby. Jesus."

She handed me her purse, took off her coat, and said, "Okay."

Ms. Ruby climbed into the bed we had made for her. Then she looked at the mattresses lined up against the gym wall and said, "Good night, Jesus. Ho, ho, ho!"

On Christmas morning, all of us ate breakfast together. Then we got into the van and took the men back. As they climbed out of the van, Ms. Ruby said to each one, "Bye, Jesus. Ho, ho, ho." To which every single one of them responded, "Bye, Ruby," or "Merry Christmas, Ruby."

On our way back to church, we passed three men who were experiencing homelessness in the neighborhood around our church. I was so focused on the road that I missed seeing them, but not Ms. Ruby. She pointed and said to me, "Buddy, Jesus, Jesus is there. See Jesus?"

I stopped, looked to my right, and saw Steve, Alan, and John, three friends experiencing homelessness. We still had food left from our Christmas breakfast, so we invited our friends into the van and headed to the church, where all of us shared breakfast leftovers.

Jesus was there.

Experiencing Advent

Advent truly is the most wonderful time of the year for me. It is a season of preparation, anticipation, waiting, longing, and celebration; you can smell the scent of hope and new beginnings in the air. Every year I crave its arrival more and more.

For the past few years, I've noticed that I have developed a routine for entering into the new Christian liturgical year. On the first Sunday of Advent, as soon as I wake up, I sit up in my bed and release a very long exhale. This moment represents my receiving the invitation Jesus extends when he says, "Come to me, all you who are struggling hard and carrying heavy loads, and I will give you rest" (Matthew 11:28 CEB). For me, the moment is more than the physical process of letting my diaphragm and the muscles between my ribs relax and reduce the space taken up by air in my chest cavity. It is spiritually breathing out all the pain, suffering, and hopelessness I have experienced within and without during the year past, preparing space so I can breathe in more of life with Christ in the days to come.

My Advent routine does not end with this moment of exhale and inhale. Once I'm up with a fresh cup of coffee in hand, I light a candle, pull up the music playlist on my phone, and listen to a version of a Charles Wesley hymn, "Come, Thou Long-Expected Jesus." My favorite version is by

Sandra McCracken and Derek Webb. I usually play the song a few times until I find myself getting lost in deep longing and prayer as I sing along.

> Come, thou long-expected Jesus,
> born to set thy people free;
> from our fears and sins release us,
> let us find our rest in thee.
> Israel's strength and consolation,
> hope of all the earth thou art;
> dear desire of every nation,
> joy of every longing heart.[2]

Advent is a time when we pause to remember and celebrate the birth of Jesus Christ. It is a time to celebrate with grateful hearts the incarnation of love in Jesus. We journey through the weeks of Advent with awe and wonder at the unfathomable love of God, that God would choose to pour Godself into the world through Jesus, in order for us truly to know that love and to be liberated to experience new life. We experience a different life orientation that shapes our vision, speech, thoughts, and actions, and we seek to bear witness to such love long after Christmas has come and gone.

Advent also is a time when we name and remember our longing for and need of forgiveness, restoration, and redemption in the present day, waiting for Christ to come again in final victory. In the meantime, as we wait, Jesus calls us into the world to participate in acts of compassion, preparing the way for God's love to be known by all who are in need of hearing the good news, having their sight restored, and experiencing freedom.

The most transformative understanding of Jesus that I have encountered—through Scripture and through the relationships I have formed in following the Great Commandment to love God and neighbor (Matthew 22: 36-40 CEB) —is of his mission to set us free.

A New Way of Seeing

I learned from Ms. Ruby that we often miss Jesus because we haven't correctly understood how God is in our midst. As we study Jesus' teachings and allow the stories to soak into our hearts and minds, we begin to notice the light of Jesus in every person we encounter, no matter how dim or bright that light may be. Too often, we are caught up in the circumstances that shaped the stories of people whom Jesus opens the door for us to love, which can blind us from the light that is in everyone. We see in the ministry and teachings of Jesus that loving our neighbors means meeting people where they are. It means looking through their circumstances to see who they are and how God is inviting us to be a reflection of unconditional and accepting love in their life. This is the good news that frees, brings peace, and heals.

If we are able to see the truth that we were loved by God before we took our first breath, and that there is nothing that can separate us from God's love, then we will be more able to love and accept each other. We will also be able to help others see the light in themselves.

This new way of seeing has the power to remove the oppressive weight of our guilt and shame, to heal our brokenness, and to free us from the fears that hinder relationship. Changing our perspective, seeing others as God sees them, has the power to reconcile communities that are fractured by the sins of racism, sexism, elitism, and any other "ism" that denies the sacred worth or dignity of others. If we truly see God in our midst, we will be able to love our neighbors and ourselves in ways that free, empower, and restore our communities and us.

I am thankful for Ms. Ruby's spiritual wisdom, which enabled her to see plainly what we often miss. She simply saw our guests, who were strangers, as Jesus sees them, as friends. And since they were friends, she made sure they had food to eat and a place to stay. She was willing to step out of her comfort zone and invite others to pay attention so we didn't miss an opportunity to love and be loved by Jesus. That night when we hosted Room in the Inn, God worked through Ms. Ruby in a way that liberated me to a new way of life, thought, and practice.

Jesus as Liberator

The Scripture reading at the beginning of this chapter is one of the most profound passages portraying Jesus as liberator. At the synagogue, Jesus appropriated the prophecy of Isaiah 61 as an interpretation of his ministry, stating that he was sent to preach the gospel or good news to those whose life chances were stifled economically, socially, physically, or mentally. Just as this was Jesus' mission, we too are sent to offer words that heal, empower, and liberate.

Usually at the church I attend, the presiding minister pronounces the following benediction with great enthusiasm at the close of the service: "And remember, you can do all things... through Christ... who strengtheeeeeeeens us!" Though some may think the benediction is trite or a simple platitude, it is actually quite powerful. Our church community is filled with a diverse group of people from all circumstances and walks of life, battling hard realities such as broken relationships, addiction, financial strains, homelessness, pressures to perform, unemployment, and illness. Thus, it is quite helpful and encouraging to be reminded that we can win the battle, that though our problems aren't going away when we walk out the door, we will be sustained by God as we follow Jesus. I find that the repetition of those words every Sunday does something to me. As they soak in, week by week, they begin to inform how I perceive my own experience and how I encourage those I relate to in the community.

One day, a project I was working with invited a local jewelry artist to come and lead a jewelry-making workshop at the homeless shelter. I went from table to table, along with the interns who worked with me, encouraging everyone to participate. We were able to get a few to reluctantly come and try. We kept saying, "You won't know if you like it or what you're capable of doing until you try."

One man stared blank-faced at the supplies placed before him and said to me, "Pastor, I can't do this. I ain't never done anything like this before."

"What do you mean, friend?" I quickly retorted. "You can do anything you put your mind to. You'll see. Believe."

I then walked away and joined in the activities myself. By the end of the workshop, every person who sat at the table had created at least one bracelet. Their faces showed such a sense of accomplishment, joy, and delight. One person even said, "This was so much fun, I almost forgot I was at the shelter."

When I was at a community festival a few months later, a gentleman walked up to me and asked, "Pastor, do you remember me?" His face looked vaguely familiar, but I could not recall how we met. Seeing that my mind was scrolling through a Rolodex of faces, he decided to help me out.

"I was at the shelter early in the summer, and I did your jewelry class."

"Really? Wow." It was the man at the table. I honestly had not seen him since that workshop. "It is so good to see you, friend. How are you?"

"Well, I'm good. I've been meaning to get down to the shelter to talk to you. I wanted to let you know when you told me at the table I could do anything I put my mind to, something happened *in* me.

"When I got up the next morning, I started hustling to find a decent place to live so I could get a good job. I was only at that shelter for two nights. Now I work for this nonprofit as the groundskeeper. Thank you for that class and for the love. I'm doing real good."

Through that experience and others over my time at the homeless shelter, I learned that just as we hunger for bread and thirst for water, we also hunger and thirst to encounter beauty within and without. All of us long to create, co-create, and contribute to this world. I feel that this is an innate need, born of God, and the experience is meant not just for a privileged few but for all.

One of the powerful ways Jesus liberates us is to affirm the wonderful truth that we are all distinctly created and endowed with gifts to participate in God's work in the world! The empowering word of God, expressed in love around an art table, was enough for my friend to maintain hope and persevere until he found the new life God and he desired for him to have.

Joining Jesus in His Mission

Daily, Jesus invites us to come and see what he is up to in the world. In fact, some of my favorite passages in the Gospels are the call narratives, in which Jesus invites the disciples to come and follow him. What has struck me about the call narratives is not that Jesus intentionally gathered to himself a team of men and women with whom he could teach his mission and equip them to live it out; that was a normal thing for rabbis to do during Jesus' day. What I find so compelling about these stories is the peculiar nature of the people he called. They were not the ones who seemed qualified for the job educationally, socially, politically, or even ethically.

I have always been somewhat of a formalist, believing that before one was hired for a position, one needed to be qualified and rigorously prepared. Hence, these stories of Jesus' disciples intrigued me greatly. Still, Jesus called them to follow him into the cities and towns, and God was able to work in and through their lives as they surrendered their lives to God. The first disciples played a significant role in Jesus' ministry and eventually were the ones who helped spread his message to many nations. As their stories unfold through the Gospels, we learn the wisdom of Jesus' choices.

Similarly, Jesus calls us, and when we say "yes" to following, we will see God work in and through our lives. Just as Jesus invited and sent the early disciples to "fish for people," to call others to experience God's great gift of acceptance and love, Jesus invites and sends us

As I reflect on what it means to be sent, I realize that joining in Jesus' mission to liberate has allowed me to go with God to some amazing places and learn from people offering beautiful acts of love, locally, nationally, and even internationally. Each experience has increased my capacity to love and my awareness of what it looks like to prepare the way for Christ to heal and restore lives through love. Perhaps the most profound opportunity I have had to participate in Jesus' mission to liberate was when I joined what we called "the love revolution" that took place in downtown Houston, Texas.

In January 2011, I was offered an opportunity to be the project manager of a therapeutic art and economic empowerment program for men and women experiencing homelessness, called The Art Project, Houston (TAPH). I had been going through an intense time of praying, seeking, and listening for vocational direction, and when I finally opened myself to see what Jesus was up to in the world, the invitation came. If I took the job, my responsibility would be to create and lead a project that would use unconventional methods to empower men and women living on the streets of downtown Houston through art and the unconditional love of God.

For a number of years I had felt a strange pull toward using creativity as a means and ministry for loving God and people, especially those who were marginalized by society and even by traditional church programs. My father is a pastor and my mother is an artist, so I was always encouraged to embrace my creative self and offer my gifts in ministry. When I had done so, I had seen glimpses of what this combination could look like in ministry, and I knew deep down that it was possible. Yet, like many of us, I had a long list of "buts."

"But . . . I don't live in Houston, and I'm not sure what life would look like there."

"But . . . I am trained in sociology and theology, and I really have no official art training or experience."

"But . . . I am a youth pastor who has served mostly privileged congregations with more than enough financial resources to do what was necessary. What can I possibly know about leading an effective ministry with under-resourced and marginalized communities and churches?"

"But . . . I need a job with more financial security. I can't risk losing the comfort and possessions I've come to enjoy."

"But . . . how can I possibly add another item to my 'to do' list, and what current relationships will I have to sacrifice?"

The list went on—believe me! It was helpful to write down the buts and explore them, as they helped me discern what my real needs were and what things in my life were getting in the way of God's mission. I tried to distinguish between needs and wants so I could figure out a plan. Gradually I turned my focus from things I didn't have toward things I did have, toward trusting God to provide, and I found the process liberating.

It was freeing to know that I didn't have to be anything other than willing in order for God to work through me.

Realizing some of these truths empowered me to say yes. It also freed me to enter into relationships and encounters with Jesus that dramatically shaped and restored my own sense of self in ways I had not imagined before. In learning how to provide opportunities for the men and women I met through TAPH, and witnessing the ways in which they recreated themselves, I too was recreated.

Looking for Light

One of our guests, who like Ms. Ruby is now a close friend, has been one of my constant teachers, and she powerfully illustrates how we join Jesus' mission of bringing new life to others. I'll call her "Sunshine."

I met Sunshine during my first week with TAPH. She was standing near the church building with her roller bag and what I would learn was routine for her, a morning cup of coffee in hand. As the new kid on the block, I raised my own cup of coffee and introduced myself. She was gracious and quiet, and she didn't say more than "Okay, okay," with a little giggle and a smile. Gazing at her, I detected a "light" that seeped through the layers of heaviness and mental distress that came from being on the streets. (I later would learn that she was one of our guests at the shelter.) Her clothes on most days, like her dreads always, were matted with dirt. But under it all there was always that tiny spark of light in her eyes.

Through my job over the past four years, I've gotten to know and work closely with Sunshine. When we met, Sunshine had been living on the streets of Houston for more than ten years and attending our church for almost as long. I must have asked Sunshine once every week to join us in creating art, to which I received a very kind "No, I don't think so," with that same little giggle and a smile. Sunshine continued her daily routine around the church. (I've learned that sometimes, when there is so much inconsistency and uncertainty in people's lives, routines can help them keep some kind of sanity, some kind of control.) Meanwhile the project developed, and she got to know me better.

Our first art show at the shelter was hosted five months after we started the program, and our first audience was the other men and women at the shelter. Sunshine came for the art and the free coffee. During the show, however, I learned that she considered herself an "artist by nature" and felt very much at home in the room. One of my colleagues extended an invitation for her to join the next therapeutic art class rotation, and without hesitation she signed up.

The following week, Sunshine became a committed participant and artist in the project. She would share her favorite Scripture passage: "For God so loved the world, that he gave his only begotten Son, that whosoever believeth in him should not perish, but have everlasting life" (John 3:16 KJV). During affirmation time she would always say, "Our Father which art in heaven," reminding us all that we belonged to a creating God who gave us creative potential. Each class I watched Sunshine's light grow brighter, so much so that, by the first day of the second rotation of class, she showed up looking very different.

"Sunshine," I exclaimed, "you cut your hair!" I couldn't believe my eyes. She was wearing a fresh outfit from the clothing closet, and her hair had been washed and cut.

Sunshine was beaming. She did her little giggle and then said, "No, Lanecia. The Holy Spirit just told me it was time to take the dirt out."

That was a pivotal moment in Sunshine's life, a shifting of perspective for her. As she began to open herself up to us, everyone in the community began to see her as a light that just got brighter and brighter. I saw her do the hard work of allowing God's love to continue refining her light, through her creations in the therapeutic art class; through her worship, prayer, and meditating on the Scriptures; and through her friendship with others. I have been privileged to witness her external and internal transformation as she has begun living authentically and journeying with a community of people who love her unconditionally.

In an interview about her continuing experience of homelessness, Sunshine shared that life on the streets is

> ...not convenient. I can't get to what I want to get to living on the streets physically. The environment—we are not in a rich environment; we are in a poor environment and The Art Project keeps us from being depressed about other things. Some of us may not have enough to go to McDonald's every day, and I am used to that. Art kind of helps, you know. I feel a little better doing something. I don't feel so depressed because I don't have enough Federal Notes to go to McDonald's. It's pretty much that, you know, it helps me from getting so depressed.[3]

Sunshine's words and story show that, for her and for all of us, it may take a great deal of work to change the way we relate to others in our community and the world, but as we grow in relationship with Jesus we are empowered to do even the most challenging and seemingly impossible things.

Joining in Jesus' mission to liberate means overcoming, by the grace and unconditional love of God, our own self-doubt and fear, our need for control, and our need to fix or manipulate outcomes. Joining in Jesus' mission challenges us to understand ourselves in new ways, as disciples sent to engage the world to prepare the way for healing, for hope to be awakened, dignity restored, and the weight of guilt and shame released by the unconditional love of God.

Jesus was sent to set us free so that we may fully live. His words have as much power today as they did when he first spoke them. When we join in his mission of liberation, we will see new life springing up all around us, and we will feel it within us as well.

I find hope every day in the gospel message that what is does not have to be, and that in Jesus we see marked out for us a life full of goodness, justice, mercy, peace, forgiveness, and love. On the darkest of days, we can still find light in people and the world around us, often in the most unexpected places and moments. When we open our eyes and look for Jesus, understand his mission, and join him where he is dwelling, we will see people and places that are pregnant with new life.

What a great privilege it is to be loved by and in service with a Creator who chose to be with us, who refused to remain distant, who came in Christ so that we might truly be free.

Reflecting:
Jesus Sets Us Free

Jesus sets us free so that we may live life with joy and be light-bearers to those who need his love and hope. How can you be a light-bearer to someone who is struggling this season?

When we believe that we are enough and give what we have without worrying about our limitations or constraints, God can do the miraculous. How can living with the liberating perspective that you are enough impact the way you share your gifts and your love this Advent?

3. JESUS IS GOD WITH US

Justin LaRosa

"The virgin will conceive and give birth
to a son, and they will call him Immanuel"
(which means "God with us").

(Matthew 1:23 NIV)

Russell

Advent 2006 was an exciting time. My wife, Caroline, and I were celebrating the second birthday of our daughter, Isabella, and preparing to welcome our second child, a boy, in early March. Caroline was thirty weeks pregnant. I was in my second year working at a United Methodist church as the Director of Discipleship, which meant I was also responsible for stewarding the greeters, parkers, and all aspects of welcoming people for our seven Christmas Eve services.

When Christmas Eve arrived, Caroline began to feel bad and experienced some swelling, so she made an appointment to visit her doctor the day after Christmas. When she went to the appointment, after seeing a midwife, she was sent home and was told to take it easy and come back the following day.

Later that night, she spoke with her brother, who is a doctor, and he asked how the appointment went and how she was feeling. She described some of her symptoms, and he became very concerned. He urged Caroline to inform the doctor of her symptoms. And so, the next day, that's what she did.

Then I received the phone call. The phone call that changed everything.

Minutes after telling her doctor the symptoms, Caroline was on her way to the hospital. I raced over to admissions, and by the time I arrived she was having intense pain in her upper abdomen.

Her face was white with panic. She said it felt like she was having a heart attack, and the pain began to intensify.

Caroline was whisked out of admissions and into the ICU for a battery of tests. At first, no one could explain the pains. But soon it became clear. The baby must be induced. The doctor gave us the shocking news: the pain was from a combination of something called HELLP syndrome and preeclampsia, and my wife's life and our baby boy's life would be in imminent danger if they didn't induce labor immediately and remove him by C-section.

A few harrowing hours later, little Russell entered the world at 2 pounds, 8 ounces, and was in critical condition. Additionally, Caroline's blood pressure was so high after delivering that she could not leave her room, which meant she was unable to see our son for two very long days. And even when she did finally see Russell for the first time in the Neo-Intensive Care Unit (NICU), she couldn't hold him or touch him because of his fragility and the need for him to remain in the incubator, which would be his home for seven long weeks.

Russell is healthy and happy now. But in the hospital, just days after celebrating the birth of Jesus, we watched as our baby boy was clinging to life and began to experience more deeply what the phrase meant: "God with us."

Meeting Us Where We Are

Our God is not indifferent. God is relational and benevolent and draws us to love through grace. God's love is deep and rich and extends to all persons and creation, but it does not mean we get everything we want or that our life circumstances will turn out in our favor. And though our story happened to end well, I realize that many stories don't and I am sensitive to that truth. No matter what your life is like, it is my belief that God travels with us in all circumstances.

One remarkable thing I've found about following Jesus is that God fully understands and knows us to the core—the good, bad, and ugly; our darkness and our light. And God can hold them all. Our faith affirms the paradox that Jesus was not just fully divine but fully human. The church calls this paradox the Incarnation. God came to earth. He knew about pain. He knew about waiting, not knowing, and being afraid. He knew about joy. And he knew he was sent so that we, in turn, would be sent. This is good news indeed.

In our case, God was with us before and after Russell's delivery. When we received the grim word from Caroline's doctor that she must be induced or both her life and Russell's would be in danger, I was utterly shocked. Somehow, though, I remained calm and present with my wife. We prayed. We called our faith community and family. One of our pastors rushed to the hospital to pray with us just prior to our going in for the delivery. Our friends and small group members prayed from afar.

In the first few weeks following Russell's birth, our family was scared. We confronted the possibility that Russell could die, as well as the probability that he could have longer-term developmental issues as a result of being born prematurely. With the benefit of hindsight, we have come to understand God's presence with us, through Jesus, in a variety of ways.

Jesus Is God With Us in the Pain

> *When Jesus saw her weeping, and the Jews who had come along with her also weeping, he was deeply moved in spirit and troubled. "Where have you laid him?" he asked. "Come and see, Lord," they replied. Jesus wept. (John 11:33-35 NIV)*

Pain is a fundamental reality of our human experience, and the truth is that most of us want to avoid it at all costs. Caroline and I have endured our share of pain, heartache, and longing, but we weren't prepared for the kind of emotional ache we encountered those first few days after Russell's birth. Caroline's blood pressure remained sky-high, and the healthcare team was having trouble bringing it down. And though her physical pain had been considerable prior to delivery, it didn't compare to the intense longing she experienced after Russell was born because of her inability to touch, see, or smell her little boy.

Rewind to two years earlier. . . . It was Advent, and we were in that same hospital. Caroline went into labor with our first child, Isabella. I ventured into the hospital gift shop and bought an angel pin for her to have during the delivery, to serve as a reminder of God with us. She asked me to wear the pin, so that when she needed to focus on her breathing and regulate her pain she could gaze at it. It worked, and to this day she can describe the way it allowed her to focus and experience Christ's presence.

Two years later, back in the hospital for Russell's delivery, the item I most desperately wanted was that angel pin so Caroline could have some tangible representation of God's love during her pain. But there was neither time to go home nor time for someone to bring it to us. So I hightailed it to the hospital gift shop. When I arrived, I scurried around the store like a hungry animal looking for food. I circled the store a couple of times, but to no avail. I couldn't find an angel pin.

When I asked at the counter, the volunteer cashier answered, "I'm sorry, but they are out of stock." That was when my emotions took over. Tears began to flow as I grappled with the notion that I might come back to Caroline empty-handed. I apologized to the cashier, and I explained our situation and the reason why I so desperately wanted that angel pin.

As I spoke, another volunteer approached, saying she had overheard my story. She wore an angel pin and said she would like to give it to me and my wife. I tried to give her some money, but she refused, saying it was her gift to our family. And she named a truth: it wasn't just an ordinary angel pin; it was a tangible expression of God with us.

Jesus Is God With Us in Uncertainty and Fear

> *So do not fear, for I am with you; do not be dismayed, for I am your God. I will strengthen you and help you; I will uphold you with my righteous right hand.*
>
> *(Isaiah 41:10 NIV)*

When I first went to the NICU to visit my newborn son, I was startled. It was not a peaceful place. The constant ringing of bells and alarms reminded me of a casino, with its flashing lights, hustle and bustle, and constant noise. I understand the hospital has since remodeled its NICU, most likely in an effort to create a more tranquil atmosphere. At that time, though, I can assure you it was anything but a place of serenity. It was noisy, chaotic, and in a constant state of activity and motion.

The NICU had a number of different sections, and my recollection is that each wing had five to seven babies with one or two nurses assigned. The space was not big enough to accommodate the number of babies in incubators, along with nurses, family members, and visitors. It was cramped and confining. The lights were halogen, so I experienced the space as stark, artificial, and depressing.

Caroline had not yet visited Russell, so I did my best to prepare her for what she was about to experience—not just the noise and chaos, but the shocking image of our baby boy, bare chest heaving rapidly with breathing tubes in his mouth, a feeding tube protruding from his nose, and webs of cords attached to his fragile body. As I wheeled Caroline down to the NICU, wearing her angel pin, I told her how much I loved her.

When we arrived at the entrance to the NICU, we were informed the staff was doing a shift change and we would have to wait. We waited silently in the hallway. The tension built with every minute. When they finally let us in and we approached the incubator, Caroline's bearing shifted noticeably. Her fear of the future and anxiety about the road ahead were as clear as the glass that separated us from our son. She stood up and removed a blanket that was covering the incubator so she could look at him.

Neither of us paid much attention to that blanket, but later it came to represent another signpost that Jesus was God with us. We learned that it wasn't just any blanket; it had been knitted with love and prayer by a group of women from a nearby church, one with which I was very familiar. Their quilting ministry, made up of women ranging from their fifties to their eighties, met two times a month to knit blankets for every child entering the NICU.

We peered into the glass, unable to touch, hold, smell, or caress Russell. We couldn't make out all of his face, because he was wearing some sort of purple foam sunglasses that were part of his treatment for jaundice. The glass separating us from him served as a protective barrier that sustained his life. We could see him with our eyes; love him with our hearts, minds, and souls; feel connected to him through our shared DNA. Yet at the same time there was a deep feeling of separation and helplessness. We were scared.

I don't pretend to know the full being and nature of God, but I got an inkling of what it might have felt like when God sent Jesus into our glass enclosure. Though the thought is inadequate and cannot approach an understanding of God's being, we did get a brief glimpse of God's penetrating love for us. We wanted to climb into that incubator and be with Russell, offering a healing presence that would allow him to thrive.

As it turned out, a couple showed us the way in. Soon after our encounter with Russell, we met parents who had a little boy a few incubators down. At birth, the boy had weighed just over one pound, and he had been in the hospital since Halloween. Though the couple lived forty-five minutes away, they were regular company in the NICU. As we got to know each other, they shared with us their experience, strength, and hope with regard to their son. One day, when I looked into their son's incubator, I noticed something that looked like a hand snuggled up with their boy. The couple told us it was The Zaky, a cloth hand designed to bring the parents inside the incubator to be with their child. Parents slept with The Zaky, then placed it inside the incubator, so the baby would learn to recognize their scent. After explaining, they told us they wanted to give us their extra Zaky.[1]

We gratefully accepted The Zaky, then slept with it and brought it back to Russell's incubator. That thoughtful gift gave us a way to be present with Russell when we couldn't touch him or be at the hospital. For Russell and for us, The Zaky was a tangible reminder of God's boundless love that sent Jesus to the world to be with us in our uncertainty and fear.

Jesus Is God With Us in Waiting

> *"And when you pray, do not be like the hypocrites, for they love to pray standing in the synagogues and on the street corners to be seen by others. Truly I tell you, they have received their reward in full. But when you pray, go into your room, close the door and pray to your Father, who is unseen. Then your Father, who sees what is done in secret, will reward you." (Matthew 6:5-6 NIV)*

Seven weeks isn't a long time to wait; in the scheme of things, it's a blip. Yet waiting seven weeks to bring baby Russell home felt like a lifetime.

As we confronted the uncertainty of Russell's health, God drew me to a sacred space to meditate and prepare, a waiting room of sorts. The hospital's chapel is a quiet, beautiful, and reverent space. There I felt connected to God's steadfast presence and somehow was better able to persevere. My times in the chapel began with verbal prayers and brief Scripture reading, then transitioned to a different kind of prayer rooted in silence.

Silence prepares us to receive more fully God's presence. But to enter into the way of silence, we must be willing to wait and endure repetitive inner noise. Silence has been an important part of my walk with Christ. Jesus told the disciples in the Sermon on the Mount not to babble their prayers in front of others, but to go into a room, shut the door, and pray to their Father in secret.

I'm not sure the disciples had a room to enter or a door to close. Some ancient Christians used the Scripture to mean that Jesus invites us to pray without words. They called it "prayer of the heart." Early in my faith walk, I traveled to a monastery where I learned about Christian contemplation, solitude, and the spiritual practices of Lectio Divina, Centering Prayer, and the St. Ignatius method. These practices have been food for my journey, deepening my connection with Christ and helping me learn how to wait upon the Lord.

Advent invites us into waiting. Psalm 46:10 (NIV) states, "Be still, and know that I am God." I have found that cultivating inner stillness is a difficult practice, particularly during busy seasons of life such as Advent and Christmas. There is so much hustle and bustle during the Christmas season. Our way of life doesn't seem to allow room for creating margin, creating stillness, and waiting.

Some people avoid silence because they are afraid of what they might find there. I want to suggest that silence is yet another place in which we experience God with us. Rooting oneself in the present is a struggle, even though it is the very place where God is most available to us. Cultivating a disciplined practice of silence or prayer without words helps ground us in the moment and commune with God. Yet even with regular practice, it is a lifelong journey to live more of our moments there.

When as a community we sit and wait, knowing without words that God is present, we are able to enter into prayer with a spirit of hopeful anticipation. Waiting is exactly what we do in Advent. Waiting in silent prayer creates receptiveness for the gift of Jesus. Waiting prayerfully was what got Caroline and me through the most difficult seven weeks of our lives.

Jesus Is God With Us in Times of Joy

> *A woman giving birth to a child has pain because her time has come; but when her baby is born she forgets the anguish because of her joy that a child is born into the world. So with you: Now is your time of grief, but I will see you again and you will rejoice, and no one will take away your joy.*
> (John 16:21-22 NIV)

In our experience with Russell, joy didn't come right after his birth, but we experienced moments along the way. We felt it when, for the first time, we could place a hand in the incubator and gently cover Russell's little body. We felt it when we could actually hold him on our chests outside the incubator. And we certainly felt it when I pushed the hospital doors open with Caroline, Isabella, and Russell to go home. All of us had been changed by the pain, the uncertainty and fear, the waiting, and the joy.

I am currently helping launch a second campus for a church in a city that is undergoing revitalization. Last Advent we decided to shift what we did the day before Christmas Eve. Instead of holding a worship service, we decided to go caroling. We named our event "Carols in the City," and we mapped out a route that included the bus station, which we intentionally selected because it was a place where homeless people often gathered.

As we sang that day, we picked up many people who decided to join us along the way. When we arrived at the bus station, we sang a Christmas carol and then formed a large circle. People waiting for buses watched with curiosity. Others, who appeared to be homeless, circled around and listened as we said a prayer and read the Gospel account of Jesus' birth. After the reading, one of the men walked to the middle of the circle and began to weep. He lifted his hands into the air, praying and praising Jesus' life, death, and resurrection. In that powerful moment, in an unexpected place, the man not only experienced the joy of Jesus but gave joy to those of us in the circle. He exuded gratitude, not for our presence, but for what Christ meant to him.

In the Gospel of John, Jesus told the disciples he had to go away and would no longer be with them physically. He used the metaphor of a woman forgetting her pain during childbirth because it was blotted out by the joy of the birth. Jesus knew the disciples would experience pain because he was to die a gruesome death on the cross. Yet he also knew their grief would eventually be transformed into joy because of his resurrection. For Caroline and me, Jesus' metaphor had special meaning.

This past year, prior to Christmas break, Russell and his classmates made Christmas cards for their parents. When Russell delivered and narrated the card to us on Christmas Eve, we received a gift not to be forgotten. Russell's card didn't depict Santa Claus, Christmas presents, or a manger. Instead, he had drawn a crimson and orange sunrise with a large cross. The cross had a purple shroud draped over it and was flanked by two smaller crosses. At the top of the cross, Russell had written a note: "Der God, thak you for my life."

Amen.

Sent

> *"You are the light of the world. A town built on a hill cannot be hidden. Neither do people light a lamp and put it under a bowl. Instead they put it on its stand, and it gives light to everyone in the house. In the same way, let your light shine before others, that they may see your good deeds and glorify your Father in heaven." (Matthew 5:14-16 NIV)*

The Twelve-Step community echoes the essence of this Scripture with their saying about sobriety, "If you want to keep it, you have to give it away." They believe that because you have developed a relationship with a higher power that has enabled you to receive the gift of sobriety, then you must come alongside others and support them in that same quest. As community members are sent to sojourn with others, they keep their lives of sobriety. For people in recovery from addiction, giving it away so that they can keep it is a matter of life and death.

The Scripture says, in essence, that because you have experienced the grace of God in Jesus Christ, who is God with you in the pain, in the uncertainty and fear, in the waiting, and in the joy, you must let your light shine. Just as Jesus was sent to us, we are sent to embody God's love to others.

In the case of our experience with Russell, we saw incarnational signposts in a volunteer's angel pin, a knitting group's blanket, a caring couple's Zaky, a hospital's waiting room, and a little boy's Christmas card. Each of the people involved, as in our Scripture, offered their good deeds and most certainly glorified our Father in heaven.

And so we ask, To whom am I sent? And for what?

Only you and your faith community can answer those questions. But make no mistake, God is calling you and me to be signposts for others. We are to take our life experiences and allow God to transform them so that we can become the hands and feet of Christ.

The answers to those questions may lead you or your family to find ways to be sent. For us, after our experience with Russell, we wanted to give back, even if it was in a small way. We yearned to express our gratitude to God for all those people who were God with us. We wanted to be sent to those experiencing the shock and awe of a trip to the NICU. So we initiated a small NICU ministry at our church. We created a basket with a Zaky, two books on prematurity, and a prayer shawl woven in love. The ministry has allowed us to position ourselves as some of God's signposts to others.

Our God is not indifferent. Our God, through Jesus, is relational and benevolent. Our God draws us to love through grace. Be with Christ and be sent.

Reflecting: Jesus Is God With Us

Jesus was sent to be "God with us" always—in our pain, in our waiting, and in our rejoicing. Have you ever struggled to believe this? How have you experienced the presence of God in your life?

What would it look like for you to live out the reality that Jesus is "God with us" this Advent? How can you allow God's light to radiate through you—even in the darkest places?

4. JESUS BRINGS NEW LIFE

Rachel Billups

The hand of the LORD was on me, and he brought me out by the Spirit of the LORD and set me in the middle of the valley; it was full of bones. . . . He asked me, "Son of man, can these bones live?" I said, "Sovereign LORD, you alone know."

(Ezekiel 37:1, 3 NIV)

The Christmas Tree Skirt

I was running down the hallway when she caught me by the arm.

"I have something for you," declared Donna. I was late for young adult Sunday school class, but she was grinning from ear to ear, so I knew it must be good.

"You have to open it," she gently urged me. She placed a wrapped gift in my hands, and I quickly but carefully unwrapped the paper to discover a hand-knit Christmas tree skirt, white with red trim.

"It's beautiful!" I declared. "Thank you! Thank you, Donna."

I gave her a hug and headed to Sunday school class, careful not to let Donna see my frustration. Just the week before I had preached a sermon about a different Christmas tree skirt.

In the sermon I had described a trip my husband Jon and I had taken to a home improvement store to purchase piping for a youth group banner. As with most of our shopping experiences, we were determined to get in and get out as quickly as possible. No more than two steps in, I noticed that the Christmas decorations were out on display. The display was impressive and so I moved in that direction, mesmerized by the glitter and glamour of the decorations. That's when it hit me: I needed a new Christmas tree skirt.

Forgetting why I had come in the first place, I looked up and down the aisles until I found the tree skirts. Although there were several, one caught my eye: fancy but not gaudy. I pictured that tree skirt under my Christmas tree and knew it would be perfect!

As I stood there, gazing at it, my husband came around the corner. Without looking at me or the tree skirt, he grabbed the price tag and exclaimed, "Forty bucks!"

"But, honey," I whined, "I need it."

Of course, I didn't need that tree skirt, so I decided not to buy it. Instead, it became a great illustration for my sermon, in which I railed against the effects of consumerism in the church and our tendency to confuse our needs for our wants. I didn't need a new tree skirt; what I needed was to focus on Jesus during the Advent and Christmas season. And Donna had missed the point.

Why didn't Donna understand? How could she have done the very opposite of what I had preached? Had she even been listening? I may have wanted a fancy new tree skirt, but I didn't need one, or at least I didn't think I did.

I didn't know it, but through Donna's gift of a tree skirt, God was starting something new: new in Donna, new in the church, and new in me. It was a revolution of sorts, and it didn't begin with perfect theology or great insight into the ills of consumerism. No, it began with the simplest of gifts. It began with a tree skirt. And the tree skirt began with the people God had placed in the pews, right there in front of me.

Dry Bones

I met Donna while serving as an associate pastor at Duke's Chapel United Methodist Church. Duke's Chapel, regularly confused with Duke University's Chapel, was a small, formerly rural church located on the north side of Durham, North Carolina. Although Duke's Chapel had experienced many decades of ministering to the community, the community had rapidly changed—economically, racially, socially—and now some of the folks at Duke's Chapel had developed a vision problem. Tired, sometimes angry, and a little bit confused, they did not see themselves as a gift of God.

I believe pastors can bring incredible vision to churches, but we also can damage people's vision. At Duke's Chapel, I remember sitting in a "visioning" meeting with the senior pastor, attempting to scare our tiny congregation into ministry. We projected a photo of the church sign, digitally edited to read *Closed*. It was not one of my proudest moments, but it made the point. We were losing ground and losing it fast. We did not see ourselves as a resource God could use to do something new; more often, we thought of ourselves as dry bones.

We would not have been the first group of dry bones. In the Book of Ezekiel, the valley of dry bones is one of the most terrifying and awe-inspiring images in Scripture. This encounter of Ezekiel with God shows that there can be hope in some of the most hopeless situations. God's people had been driven into exile and were dispersed throughout the land. Ezekiel, a priestly prophet of God, found himself living in exile under a weakening Assyrian Empire. In Chapter 37 we find that Ezekiel was caught up in some kind of spiritual state; he was in the very presence of God.

> The hand of the LORD was on me, and he brought me out by the Spirit of the LORD and set me in the middle of a valley; it was full of bones. He led me back and forth among them, and I saw a great many bones on the floor of the valley, bones that were very dry.
>
> (Ezekiel 37:1-2 NIV)

To Ezekiel, the scattered bones represented the people of God—exiled, scattered throughout the nations. It must have been a gruesome scene. I can't imagine what Ezekiel must have been thinking: What has happened here? Who were these people? What did they do to deserve such a death?

When I read Ezekiel 37, I can't help but remember pictures of genocide that I've seen, from the gas chambers of Auschwitz to the rivers of Rwanda. Images such as these fill our hearts and minds with a sense of fear, darkness, and hopelessness. Though certainly not in the same awful category as those pictures, it's not too much of a stretch to think of some church images: from decaying cathedrals in Europe to increasingly empty pews throughout the United States, the church sometimes can seem like a pile of dry bones.

In my denomination, The United Methodist Church, the median age for ordained elders (a category of clergy) is now fifty-six.[1] According to research by the Barna Group, only 20 percent of millennials say that church is important to them.[2] These statistics aren't the only indication that churches are shrinking and closing, but they do point to a church that has much in common with Ezekiel's desolate vision of dry bones: a people scattered, at moments lifeless, in places seemingly hopeless.

And yet, if we keep reading Ezekiel 37, the valley of bones is not a vision of death. It is a vision ripe with the possibilities of new life. Mentor and friend Mike Slaughter often says, "God does God's best work in cemeteries!" Even when we think death is imminent, even when we see no signs of life, we can rest assured that God is at work.

In Ezekiel 37:3, God asked Ezekiel a profound and prophetic question: "Son of man, can these bones live?" Ezekiel, gazing out over the bones, could have responded with a reasonable "no" or a self-righteous "yes." Instead he said, "Sovereign Lord, you alone know." Maybe Ezekiel was skirting the question, or maybe in face of such overwhelming despair he felt the only sensible response was to place responsibility back in God's hands. If the bones were going to live, it would be because of God and the power of God's Spirit.

We at Duke's Chapel asked ourselves the same question: Can these bones live? Actually, our question was phrased a bit differently: Will we be able to pay our staff? What happens if the boiler busts? Can we replace the windows in the parsonage? Will our congregation ever grow? Can we attract more young families?

We wanted to experience new life, but we didn't know how. We bought the lie that a flurry of activity centered on ourselves would make us feel alive, but all it brought was exhaustion. From church bazaars to bake sales, we did things to keep the lights on, but they certainly didn't feel like new life. Finally, peering into our future, I replied as Ezekiel did: "God, you alone know."

The crazy thing about Ezekiel's vision was that God didn't let him off the hook. Even though Ezekiel's reply was based on sound theology, God wanted him to participate in the work.

> Then he said to me, "Prophesy to these bones and say to them, 'Dry bones, hear the word of the LORD! This is what the Sovereign LORD says to these bones: I will make breath enter you, and you will come to life. I will attach tendons to you and make flesh come upon you and cover you with skin; I will put breath in you, and you will come to life. Then you will know that I am the Lord.'" (Ezekiel 37:4-6 NIV)

Sometimes I want God to do something amazing and miraculous in the church, but I want God to do it without me: "God, make it happen, but don't expect me to give my blood, sweat, and tears!" But God doesn't let us off the hook, any more than he did Ezekiel. God worked through Ezekiel to bring the bones back to life, and he expects the same of us.

Words are powerful! Solomon in all his wisdom declared, "The tongue has the power of life and death, / and those who love it will eat its fruit" (Proverbs 18:21 NIV). Too often we underestimate the power of our words in the church. I'm not talking about the words we use in the hour when we gather for worship. I'm talking about the words we use in the parking lot, in online posts, in casual conversations.

I remember standing in the sanctuary of Duke's Chapel with a parishioner who said to me, "This church is never going to change! We haven't changed for the last twenty-five years, and we're not going to start now!" Those words communicated a vision (or lack of vision) that the person believed to be true for herself and the church. New life would only begin when we started talking about ourselves differently.

I know what some of you may be thinking: That sounds an awful lot like Stuart Smalley, the obsessively optimistic character who appeared in then-comedian Al Franken's book *I'm Good Enough, I'm Smart Enough, and Doggone It, People Like Me!* (New York: Dell Publishing, 1992). Unlike Stuart, though, the people in our congregation were doing more than just flattering themselves. All of us started speaking words of encouragement over one another, and it worked.

New Life

Remember Donna and the Christmas tree skirt? Donna had some incredible gifts. She could make things with her hands, she could offer warm hospitality, and frankly she could talk your ear off (at the same time making you feel like the most loved person in the world). Donna was one of the people we started speaking encouragement over. We said, "Donna, did you know that you could use your gifts to change people's lives?" And so she did.

She helped start a ministry called the Traveling Tea Party (no, not that Tea Party). Honestly, we borrowed the idea from another church. A group of retirees would get together and bake goodies, then take them to nursing homes, assisted living units, and the homes of people who couldn't make it to church. Rooms would be filled with the smells of bundt cake or chess pie. (Forget being on a diet that week!) The retirees would engage in conversation with their peers.

I loved to tag along because it was like opening the pages of a history book. These men and women would talk about the Civil Rights Movement, changes in education, and how the city of Durham had been transformed over the last fifty years. They would laugh with one another, cry with one another, and then pray for one another.

I learned that it's not just pastors who are called to be Ezekiels; everyone has the power to speak new life over dead bones. I also learned that the people of the church were not the only ones with a vision problem. When I first arrived at Duke's Chapel, I had thought it was my job to fix the church, to make it happen, to do the ministry; but quickly I realized God had given me a group of people with incredible gifts in their hands. I had to be willing not only to speak words of life myself, but to allow others to speak words of life. We preacher types can get so consumed with doing ministry that we forget to empower others in using their gifts for God's kingdom purposes. God had not called me to do the entire ministry; no, God had called me to equip and empower God's people to do ministry.

What happens when a church starts believing that God has given them gifts that they need to share with the community and the world? New life happens! Resurrected life happens! Ezekiel, when confronted with dead bones, had a choice. He could choose to believe what he saw, what appeared to be true; or he could obey God and speak a word of encouragement, a word of life, over bones that already were dead. What did Ezekiel choose? New life!

> So I prophesied as I was commanded. And as I was prophesying, there was a noise, a rattling sound, and the bones came together, bone to bone. I looked, and tendons and flesh appeared on them and skin covered them, but there was no breath in them. (Ezekiel 37:7-8 NIV)

God has given all of us the privilege of standing in the valley, and we, like Ezekiel, have a choice. We can believe that the bones will live, or we can refuse to believe. Sometimes we get so discouraged with problems that are right in front of us that we forget the power of God. What would happen if we, like Ezekiel, began speaking prophetic and encouraging words over ourselves? What a rattling sound there would be! Suddenly people who had never engaged in ministry or barely attended church might start giving their lives to Jesus' kingdom work in our communities, cities, and world.

Using Our Gifts

That's exactly what happened at Duke's Chapel Church. People on the margins started engaging in ministry. Suddenly they believed that God could use their ordinary gifts. One of the gifts that many in the church possessed was the gift of hospitality. When it came to new people coming to visit, the people at Duke's Chapel would always make them feel welcome.

We had a nominal relationship with Urban Ministries of Durham, one of the local homeless shelters, in which we gave the organization money but did little to build relationships with the people. So we started to dream. Those dreams turned into monthly parties.

We discovered that the homeless shelter had nine housing units for children, and because those families were in crisis they had few resources with which to celebrate milestones in the kids' lives: birthdays, holidays, accomplishments in school. Our dreams turned into a regular celebration with the families at the shelter, and whether it was Valentine's Day or birthdays, we began to celebrate milestones with those families. We didn't buy the children presents, but many in the church made awesome food, and we talked with them. And it wasn't just the homeless population at the shelter. We started working with men and women on the street: engaging in conversation, advocating on their behalf, and inviting them into our church family.

One year we decided to give up our Thanksgiving Day family celebration so we could celebrate Thanksgiving with our brothers and sisters who found themselves homeless. We asked them to spread the word about the party and invite anyone who was interested to celebrate Thanksgiving with us. Before we knew it, we had college students, strangers, church folks, and new friends. We gathered together for a family-style meal. We prayed together, broke bread together, and shared the history of that first Thanksgiving long ago.

These were all signs of new life! But they didn't happen because of new programs; they happened because we empowered people to use the gifts God had given them. The gifts were simple: sewing, baking, driving a church van, and especially throwing parties. Jesus always talked about throwing parties. I think it's why he got himself into so much trouble. The religious elite were not good at throwing parties—at least not the kind of parties that regular people were interested in—but Jesus had a way of describing parties that changed the way people thought and acted:

> "When you give a luncheon or dinner, do not invite your friends, your brothers or sisters, your relatives, or your rich neighbors; if you do, they may invite you back and so you will be repaid. But when you give a banquet, invite the poor, the crippled, the lame, the blind, and you will be blessed. Although they cannot repay you, you will be repaid at the resurrection of the righteous." (Luke 14:12-14 NIV)

As part of our new life, we studied Scripture. We didn't always take it literally, but we did wrestle with it, asking ourselves the question, "What does God expect us to do about this?"

Our wrestling with Scripture played a huge role in transforming the way we saw our community and ourselves. We started small group Bible studies in which over half the congregation participated, meeting weekly in various homes. During one of those studies, a group met in our living room. An older gentleman in the group had been away from church most of his adult life and recently had returned. He was a person of means, and when we read Scripture it challenged him. The Bible challenged the way he lived and what he did. Finally he exclaimed, "I don't know if I can handle this Jesus stuff! This is a lot for me to take in!" We all began to realize that being disciples of Jesus came at a cost, and we were in it together—rich and poor, old and young, seasoned and brand-new to the church. Just as with that valley of dry bones, we began to see God putting us back together.

Very quickly, though, the valley of dry bones taught us another valuable lesson. Recall what happened when Ezekiel gazed upon the bones: "I looked, and tendons and flesh appeared on them and skin covered them, but there was no breath in them" (Ezekiel 37:8 NIV). The bodies still were lifeless. Why? Because they didn't have the Spirit of God in them.

Sometimes when we do missional work, we selfishly want the credit: "Look at all the wonderful things we are accomplishing! People are getting the food they need, engaging in Bible study, and going to great parties!" But that isn't the point! The point isn't to direct the community back to us, but to direct the community to the life-giving, life-saving work of Jesus Christ. Without the Spirit of God at the center of our work, it is mere busyness. And busyness does not bring life; it makes people tired and ultimately brings death. Note how God gave the fully fleshed-out bodies life?

Then he said to me, "Prophesy to the breath; prophesy, son of man, and say to it, 'This is what the Sovereign Lord says: Come, breath, from the four winds and breathe into these slain, that they may live.'" So I prophesied as he commanded me, and breath entered them; they came to life and stood up on their feet—a vast army. (Ezekiel 37:9-10 NIV).

The dead bones lived through the very breath of God. When our church attempted to do things that God did not want us to do, we got tired and cranky; but when we engaged the community in the way God was calling us to, we experienced life through the power of the Holy Spirit.

God's Economy

We all want new life. We want a new way of navigating the chaos we sometimes experience during the Advent and Christmas season. Look around you! How many of us find ourselves surrounded by church folk who are exhausted, parched, dry from their experiences of church? Even this Advent season, I find myself repeating the mantra, "I don't want to survive. I want to thrive."

It's easy to point fingers and place blame on the culture of consumerism that pervades nearly every aspect of the countdown to Christmas. Black Friday now starts on Thanksgiving Day, followed immediately by Small Business Saturday and Cyber Monday. As if that isn't bad enough, everything in the world seems to be on sale, from phones to produce, from cabbages to cars. It's not only a great time to purchase Christmas gifts, but also a time to buy things for ourselves.

The church, in an attempt to drown out the consumerism that pervades our culture, offers a smorgasbord of new experiences: Christmas plays, live Nativities, caroling, trees, wreaths, not one or two but seven new Christmas Eve services. Instead of transforming the lives of people, the church adds to the busyness and chaos. Advent becomes a time of survival, of endurance, of hanging on. Our purpose in the church is to prepare people for new life. But when church becomes one more thing added to a month of many things, we create an entire group of people who are exhausted, parched, and dry from their experience of preparation.

This is not our calling! People don't need more programs. They don't need more activities. They need purpose. The people at Duke's Chapel Church began to find their purpose; they found their God calling. It was not in the right program or even the right church activity. It was about employing their gifts so that God could transform lives.

I didn't know it, but that Sunday morning in the church hallway I was holding the key to new life right in my hands. It was the handmade Christmas tree skirt. Donna had used her simple gifts of love and hospitality, gifts that had the power to change her life, her church, and her world.

So often in the church, we want to do something big for God—as though God is not big enough. But that's not what God is looking for. That day in the hallway, I realized that God was asking me to offer myself. God wants nothing less than our whole lives. Following Jesus means turning our lives over to God—the good, the bad, and the in-between. And God wants to use all of us: our gifts, talents, and resources to change communities, cities, nations, and the world.

Isn't that what God was trying to tell us about new life, resurrected life with Jesus? It's simple! God, in the flesh, arrives in our neighborhood and becomes one of us—a retired schoolteacher, a gas station attendant, a lawyer, a plumber. No matter what our neighborhood looks like—whether there are boarded-up buildings or fancy boutiques—God sees the dry bones in all of us. There is deadness in us all, and God knows we need new life. We need God's Spirit breathed into us and our churches. Advent is the perfect time to start.

God brought new life to the world in the form of a simple gift, a baby. Instead of coming with fanfare or with political or religious power, God arrived as a poor carpenter's son, born in a stable, laid in a feeding trough. When the rest of the world anticipated power through dominance and military might, God's gift came wrapped in swaddling cloth and lying in a manager.

I wonder where Mary got that swaddling cloth. Did someone make it for her? Maybe Mary had a Donna in her life—

a woman who used her simple gift of sewing to wrap God's revolutionary gift that was born in the most ordinary of places. It makes sense to me. Why? Because that is God's economy. God empowers us to use our gifts for his kingdom purposes. God does not waste a person or a gift. Every single gift can be used to change the world.

It reminds me of Mother Teresa. By the world's standards she had nothing, but within her she had the greatest gift of all: love. Mother Teresa declared, through words and actions, "Not all of us can do great things, but we can do small things with great love."

Every year when I pull out the Christmas tree skirt, I think of Donna. These days the tree skirt doesn't make me frustrated or angry or even sentimental. These days it fills me with faith. I think about Donna's faith and the faith of Duke's Chapel Church. I think of all the things Donna did—not just sewing things, but traveling to nursing homes to visit her peers, throwing parties for homeless children, along with countless other gifts of generosity, large and small.

Donna became a prophet, as she spoke words of encouragement over everyone she met. God's love shone through her with every tree skirt, baby afghan, and homemade dessert she made. Contrary to what I had thought, Donna did not misunderstand my sermon that day; in fact, she lived it. In that tree skirt she was giving a piece of herself to me, a visual reminder of who she was and whose she was. God wanted nothing less than for Donna to give her life and gifts away.

Donna died this year, during Advent, at the ripe young age of ninety-six. Right up to the end she was still visiting people in nursing homes and throwing parties. The night she died, Donna was baking cookies for a group of Christmas carolers, filling another Advent with love, bringing new life to a world that so desperately needs it.

Can these dry bones live? You bet they can!

Reflecting: Jesus Brings New Life

Jesus came to make us new. In what ways do you need God to breathe new life into you, your circumstances, or your interactions with others? How can you make space in your life this season so that God has room to work?

Our words are powerful. Through the power of the Holy Spirit, they have the ability to bring life. How is God calling you to speak life into death with your words?

5. JESUS CHANGES EVERYTHING

Jorge Acevedo

When the right time came, God sent his Son, born of a woman…

(Galatians 4:4a NLT)

A Restless Advent Night

Two weeks before Christmas last year, I had the weirdest thought as I was drifting off to sleep: *What are the odds of being born in an exact place and in an exact time?*

Strange as it seems, this thought bounced around the gray matter in my brain as I drifted off to sleep. When I woke up the next morning it was still on my mind, so I went to Google. I typed: "Probability of being born in an exact time or place." In 0.35 seconds, 44,200,000 results appeared before me. What a great world!

Of course, I carefully studied all 44,200,000 entries, and now I have the definitive answer to this mystery of the universe. Naw, not really! I looked at a handful of the entri es, and frankly I couldn't find a philosopher, mathematician, theologian, or politician who answered the question or even had an opinion on it.

Here's what I did find: Some scientists have calculated the probability that you would exist as the unique individual you are, and the odds are 1 in 400 trillion—that's a 4 with 14 zeros after it! One author and blogger, Ali Binazir, did a long calculation that included the probability of your parents meeting, falling in love, and procreating. Then he factored in the probability of your ancestors meeting, falling in love, and procreating. Based on these figures, he estimated that the probability of your being born was…now get this…1 in 10 to the 2,685,000th power! Benazir followed his calculation with this statement:

> So what's the probability of your existing? It's the probability of 2 million people getting together—about

> the population of San Diego—each to play a game of dice with *trillion-sided dice*. They each roll the dice, and they all come up the exact same number. . . . A miracle is an event so unlikely as to be almost impossible. By that definition, I've just shown that (underline added).[1]

Wow! What my Google research did was once again to amaze me about the miracle of life. It reminded me that it wasn't just a "higher intelligence" but a Creator God who made this planet, the universe it sits in, and you and me. The God revealed in the Bible as Father, Son, and Holy Spirit lovingly crafted you in your mother's womb and cares deeply about you and all of creation.

Listen! Your birth was not an accident. Your life is a miracle. You're not one in a million. You're not even one in 7.2 billion. According to Ali Binazir, you're one in 10 to the 2,685,000th power!

Here's something else. The life of Jesus wasn't an accident either. It was an on-purpose miracle birth if there ever was one. Just as Jesus was *sent* by God to an exact time, place, and circumstance, so you and I—the people of God—are sent to make the love of Christ visible in our own time.

Jesus Changed Everything in the World

The Apostle Paul focused most of his writing on the death, burial, and resurrection of Christ. Only once did Paul write about the first hours of Jesus' life. That passage is found in his Letter to the Galatians: "When the right time came, God sent his Son, born of a woman" (Galatians 4:4a NLT).

In those words, Paul declared that Jesus' birth to Mary was not haphazard or accidental but rather was at the "right time." God sent his Son in the exact moment and to the exact parents of God's choosing. Jesus' first "advent" was on time!

There were several cultural factors that made Jesus' birth timely. Consider language, for example: Because of the exploits of Alexander the Great, the Greek language had become the common language of a very diverse world. Consider transportation: The Romans had created a road system allowing travel from Europe to Africa and Asia. Then imagine a God who wanted to spread the love of God in Christ strategically throughout the world. What would God need? A common language would help, so a maximum number of people could understand the gospel. And a system of roads would be good, so missionaries could spread the word. From a historical perspective, you could argue that God's timing for Jesus' birth was just right.

But Jesus' first Advent wasn't just on time; it was on purpose. It changed everything on this blue-green planet called Earth. Yale historian Jeroslav Pelikan wrote these words about the impact of Jesus' life:

> Regardless of what anyone may personally think or believe about him, Jesus of Nazareth has been the dominant figure in the history of Western culture for almost twenty centuries. If it were possible, with some sort of supermagnet, to pull up out of history every scrap of metal bearing at least a trace of his name, how much would be left?[2]

The impact of Jesus' influence on our world can't be measured; in fact, it's hard to think of an area that has not been affected. His teaching shaped education. His ministry changed our treatment of the poor and marginalized. His love transformed medicine. He reframed our use of money and our concepts of friend and enemy. The span of his life is even used to measure time.

Jesus changed everything! His birth was right on time and right on purpose. But let's look through a second lens at the birth of Jesus. It's a more personal lens.

Jesus Can Change Everything in *Your* World

The birth of Jesus wasn't just a historical reality two thousand years ago; it can be a spiritual reality for you today.

The first Christmas changed everything in the world; but this Christmas, Jesus can change everything in *your* world!

The Gospel of John begins with a poem. Unlike Matthew and Luke, whose accounts were more historical, the disciple who wrote John began with beautiful words and a theological account of Jesus' birth. Look at how he describes Jesus in the first chapter:

> He came into the very world he created, but the world didn't recognize him. He came to his own people, and even they rejected him. But to all who believed him and accepted him, he gave the right to become children of God. They are reborn—not with a physical birth resulting from human passion or plan, but a birth that comes from God.
>
> So the Word became human and made his home among us. He was full of unfailing love and faithfulness. And we have seen his glory, the glory of the Father's one and only Son.
>
> (John 1:10-14 NLT)

According to John, Jesus was born with a purpose: to make children of God through spiritual rebirth. Later, in John 3,

Jesus declared the necessity of being born again to enter the kingdom of God. Spiritual birth was and is the business of Jesus.

John tells us that Jesus is full of grace. Grace is God's unconditional love for us. It's the reality that there is nothing we can do that will make God love us more or love us less. God's grace will pursue us from the womb to the tomb. It is grace that draws us into a relationship with Jesus. It is grace that miraculously saves us. It is grace that keeps us in relationship with God, and it is grace that will usher us into eternity.

John also tells us that Jesus is full of truth. Jesus told hyper-religious zealots that their rule-keeping did not impress God. He told a woman who had been married five times that no man could satisfy the deepest thirst of her life. To a woman who was caught in the act of adultery, he offered a word of grace (Where are your accusers? Didn't even one of them condemn you?) and then a word of truth (Go and sin no more.).

Jesus is full of both grace and truth. You see, if Jesus were only full of grace, then our character would never be transformed; and if Jesus were only full of truth, then our hearts would never be softened. As Randy Alcorn[3] wrote: "Truth without grace breeds self-righteousness and crushing legalism. Grace without truth breeds deception and moral compromise."

Jesus was sent by God with the capacity to love without end and confront without compromise. This was the character of Jesus who was born in Bethlehem that first Christmas, and this is the character of Jesus who wants to be born anew in your life this Christmas.

A Christmas Prayer

Each of us has been born in just the right time and for just the right purpose. We have been sent by God to live lives that exemplify the love of Christ. But what does that love look like?

Though I have led or participated in Christmas Eve services for more than three decades, there is one that stands out for me. Early in my ministry at Grace Church in Southwest Florida, some of our dearest friends had a baby. A few days before Christmas, I had what I believe to be a Spirit-inspired idea. I would hold our friends' baby while I preached the Christmas Eve message announcing the birth of Jesus. By the grace of God, all three services went off without a glitch. No dirty diapers or throwing up on the preacher!

Think of what it means to declare the birth of Jesus while holding a baby. A baby is tender. A baby is gentle. A baby is powerless. In a world that seeks power, prominence, prestige, and profits, we hold the simple, tender message of Jesus' birth, and we declare it to the world.

God sent Jesus. Jesus sends us, with truth and grace. I pray that this will be the year when Jesus changes everything for you. Amen.

Reflecting: Jesus Changes Everything

Jesus' love changes everything. How has Jesus' love changed you and your life?

How can you be a part of Christ's love revolution on this planet? Where are you being sent to share Jesus' love?

Notes

Introduction

1. Phillips Brooks, "O Little Town of Bethlehem," *The United Methodist Hymnal* (Nashville: The United Methodist Publishing House, 1989), 230, stanza 4.

Chapter 1—Jesus Reconciles

1. Joseph Mohr, "Silent Night, Holy Night," *The United Methodist Hymnal,* 239, stanza 2.

Chapter 2—Jesus Sets Us Free

1. Charles Wesley, "Come, Thou Long-Expected Jesus," *The United Methodist Hymnal*, 196.
2. Charles Wesley, "Come, Thou Long-Expected Jesus," *The United Methodist Hymnal* (Nashville: The United Methodist Publishing House, 1989), 196, stanza 1.
3. Carolyn Richell, created by Lanecia Rouse, "Carolyn's Story: The Art Project, Houston", YouTube video, 3:10, July 12, 2012, https://www.youtube.com/watch?v=cJIHFTLkNrE.

Chapter 3—Jesus Is God With Us

1. Learn more about The Zacky at http://www.nurturedbydesign.com/en/thezaky/parents-hospital.php.

Chapter 4—Jesus Brings New Life

1. Lewis Center Report, "Clergy Age Trends in The United Methodist Church," 2014. http://www.churchleadership.com/clergyage/.

2. Barna Group, "5 Reasons Millennials Stay Connected to Church," September 17, 2013. https://www.barna.org/barna-update/millennials/635-5-reasons-millennials-stay-connected-to-church.html#.VY1frEZ-vP8.

Chapter 5—Jesus Changes Everything

1. Ali Binazir, "What are the chances of your coming into being." *Meanderings Over Heaven, Earth, and Mind* (blog), June 15, 2011 (3:22 p.m.), http://blogs.law.harvard.edu/abinazir/2011/06/15/what-are-chances-you-would-be-born/.

2. Jeroslav Pelikan, *Jesus Through the Centuries: His Place in the History of Culture* (New York: Yale University Press, 1999), 1.

3. Randy Alcorn, *The Grace and Truth Paradox: Responding with Christlike Balance* (Colorado Springs, CO: Multnomah Books, 2003), back cover.

Jorge Acevedo is the Lead Pastor at Grace Church, a multi-site United Methodist congregation in Southwest Florida. He is author of *Vital: Churches Changing Communities and the World* and coauthor of *The Heart of Youth Ministry*, and has been a contributor to *Circuit Rider* magazine, *Good News* magazine, and *Our Faith Today*.

(L to R) Justin LaRosa, Rachel Billups, Jorge Acevedo, Lanecia Rouse, Jacob Armstrong

Jacob Armstrong is the founding pastor of Providence Church, a five-year-old United Methodist church plant in Mt. Juliet, Tennessee, reaching 1,000 people each week. Providence's vision is to see those who are disconnected from God and the church to find hope, healing, and wholeness in Jesus Christ. Jacob is the author of *Treasure: A Stewardship Program on Faith and Money*, *The God Story*, *Upside Down*, *Loving Large*, *Interruptions*, and *The New Adapters*.

Lanecia Rouse is the author of numerous articles on Christian formation for Upper Room Ministries and Abingdon Press. She has held pastoral roles in The United Methodist and British Methodist Church, most recently as Project Manager of The Art Project, Houston, a therapeutic art ministry with those experiencing homelessness. Lanecia earned a Bachelor of Arts degree in Sociology from Wofford College and a Master of Divinity degree from Duke Divinity School. She currently lives in Houston, where she continues her ministry as a writer, artist, photographer, and workshop leader.

Justin LaRosa is a licensed clinical social worker and Deacon who leads the new ministry of Hyde Park United Methodist Church in downtown Tampa, Florida. He served for eight years as the Minister of Discipleship, working with a team of leaders to facilitate the process of organizing, training, empowering, and supporting laypersons. Justin is coauthor, with James A. Harnish, of *A Disciple's Path* and *A Disciple's Heart.*

Rachel Billups serves as the Executive Pastor of Discipleship and as part of the preaching team for Ginghamsburg Church in Tipp City, Ohio. Rachel, an Ordained Elder within The United Methodist Church, holds a Bachelor's Degree in Bible/Religion and History from Anderson University and a Master of Divinity degree from Duke Divinity School. Before joining the Ginghamsburg team, Rachel served as the lead pastor of Shiloh United Methodist, a multi-site church in Cincinnati, Ohio.

More Great Resources for This Study

DVD Features an 8- to 10- minute video for each of the five sessions with personal Advent or Christmas stories that shows how Christ sends us to liberate, to heal, to reconcile, to transform, and to bring new life.
9781501801082

Devotions Offers four weeks of daily reflections that include Scripture, personal insights, daily challenges, and prayers.
9781501801174

Leader Guide Includes session plans, discussion questions, and Scripture readings centered around the book and the videos.
9781501801068

Youth Study Book Based on the adult study and using the same DVD, the Youth Study Book gives examples relevant to youth ages 13–18.
9781501801143

Children's Leader Guide Includes ideas for both younger and older children with games, activities, crafts, and printable handouts to make the study easy to manage.
9781501801167

Printed in the USA
CPSIA information can be obtained
at www.ICGtesting.com
LVHW030029221124
797327LV00042B/1528

* 9 7 8 1 5 0 1 8 0 1 0 5 1 *